—WINE SPECTATOR's—
pocket guide to
WINE

www.winespectator.com

©2005 by Wine Spectator Press/M. Shanken Communications, Inc.

Printed in China

9   8   7   6
Digit on the right indicates the number of this printing

ISBN 0-7624-2188-6

Published by M. Shanken Communications, Inc.
387 Park Avenue South
New York, NY 10016

Book design by Chandra Hira

For subscriptions to *Wine Spectator*, please call: (800) 752-7799
in the U.S. and Canada or write:
    P.O. Box 37367
    Boone, IA 50037-0367

Visit our Web site at: www.winespectator.com

Welcome

Timothy Bell

Wine is often thought of as a sophisticated and intimidating subject, but with the right tools anyone can develop an understanding and appreciation of fine wine.

You're holding one of those tools in your hand right now. The new and expanded *Wine Spectator's Pocket Guide to Wine* will teach you the essential techniques of wine tasting through a series of simple and logical steps. You'll learn about grapes and the countries that make wine. And you'll find the information you need to get the most from wine, with advice on topics that include serving, storing, glassware, buying strategies, ordering wine in restaurants, matching food with wine and much more.

Additionally, I invite you to visit our Web site at www.winespectator.com. Of special interest is our exclusive database of over 110,000 wines—all rated for quality using *Wine Spectator*'s 100-point rating scale. Here you can research wines and compare your impressions of certain wines with those of our experts. Our Web site also offers further information on the world of wine; features on food, travel and events; and databases of award-winning restaurants, hotels and fine wine shops around the world.

I hope that this book will pique your interest in learning more about wine. To explore further, visit www.winespectatorschool.com, where you'll find fascinating courses to take you to another level of wine knowledge and appreciation.

Finally, I want to thank the editors at *Wine Spectator* for their contributions to this book—especially Thomas Matthews, original author of "The ABC's of Wine."

Cheers!

Mn R. Shl

Marvin R. Shanken
Editor & Publisher, *Wine Spectator*

The ABC's of Wine Tasting

Drinking wine is easy: Tilt glass and swallow. Really tasting wine is more of a challenge. You need the proper tools and environment, the ability to concentrate, a good memory and a vivid imagination. But after three or four glasses, the basic effect is the same either way. So why bother?

Wine lovers know that putting some effort into understanding and appreciating wine pays big dividends. Skillful tasting unlocks wine's treasures. It adds an extra dimension to the basic routines of eating and drinking, turning a daily necessity into a celebration of life.

And once in a while we get lucky. Every passionate wine lover tells the same story: a special night, close companions, an extraordinary bottle of wine. Suddenly we have the impression that what began as superficial sensory pleasure has become a profound experience. A glass of wine will never be quite the same again.

A book this short can't possibly convey everything you can learn about a wine from the way it tastes. Like any skill, serious tasting requires a combination of technique and experience. The more you do it, the better you become.

But remember that tasting is not a test. The bottom line is: Wine that tastes good to you is good wine. And no matter how advanced your technique, tasting is not an exact science. Sensitivities vary widely when it comes to flavor and aroma.

The techniques of tasting enhance the ability to perceive wine clearly. They're actually pretty simple and follow logically through a well-defined series of steps. Some of the procedures may seem unnatural or pretentious to the uninitiated, but they've been developed over centuries to achieve specific ends. After a while, they become automatic. Here's how to begin.

Set and Setting

First of all, consider the circum-
stances. Not all wines deserve
close analysis. White Zinfandel
drunk out of paper cups at a
picnic may be flavorful and
refreshing, but any attempt to
taste seriously will be wasted
effort and probably perceived
as snobbery.

To maximize both enjoyment
and understanding, serve your
wine at a dinner party with friends. Comfortable
chairs, warm light and good food create an ambiance
where the wines—and the guests—can express
themselves easily.

Looking at Wine

The first step in your examination is visual. Fill the
glass about one-third full, never more than half-full.
Pick it up by the stem. This may feel awkward or
affected at first, but there are good reasons: Holding
the glass by its bowl hides the liquid from view; fin-
gerprints blur its color; and the heat of your hand
alters the wine's temperature.

Focus in turn on hue, intensity and clarity. Each
requires a different way of looking. The color, or hue,
of the wine—orangey-red? true purple?—is best
judged by tilting the glass and looking at the wine
through the rim, to see the variation from the deepest
part of the liquid to its edges. Intensity—is the color
saturated or thin?—can best be gauged by looking
straight down through the wine from above. Clarity—
whether the wine is brilliant, or cloudy with particles—is most evident when light is shining sideways
through the glass. And don't forget simply to enjoy
the wine's color. No other liquid is as vivid and varie-
gated, or reflects light with such finesse. There's good
reason why wine's appearance is often compared to
ruby and garnet, topaz and gold.

A wine's color gives many clues to its character.
First, it can indicate the specific variety of grape
(or grapes) the wine is made from. Second, it reflects

growing conditions in the vineyard. A warm summer and dry autumn produce grapes that are fully ripe,

with a high ratio of skin to juice, resulting in dark colors. A cool summer or a rainy harvest can result in unripe or diluted grapes, which will show up in colors with lighter hues and less intensity.

Winemaking techniques can also affect color. When red wines ferment, the grape skins are left to steep in the juice, like a tea bag steeping in warm water. The coloring elements (called anthocyanins) are found in the skins, not the juice itself—even red grapes have clear juice—so the longer the skins steep, the darker the color will be.

CEPHAS/Mick Rock

Time spent in the bottle—the inevitable process of aging—also has an impact. Young red wines are full of anthocyanins, so their hues are deep. With maturity, they lighten through red to colors described as "brick" or "amber," as the anthocyanins slowly combine and fall out of suspension in the wine, creating a sediment in the bottom of the bottle.

After color observation comes the swirling. This too can feel unnatural, even dangerous if your glass is too full and your clothing brand-new. But besides stirring up the full range of colors, it prepares the wine for the next step—smelling it. The easiest way to swirl is to rest the base of the glass on a table, hold the stem between thumb and forefinger, and gently rotate the wrist. Right-handers will find a counter-clockwise motion easiest, left-handers the reverse.

Move the glass until the wine is dancing, climbing nearly to the rim. Then stop. As the liquid settles back into the bottom of the glass, a transparent film will appear on the inside of the bowl, falling slowly and irregularly down the sides in the wine's "tears" or "legs." These are simply an indication of the amount of alcohol in the wine: The more alcohol, the more tears. Remember this when you're considering whether to open another bottle.

Smelling Wine

When you stop swirling, it's time to take the next step. Agitating the wine vaporizes it, and the thin sheet of liquid on the sides of the glass evaporates rapidly, intensifying the aromas. If the glass narrows at the top, the aromas are further concentrated. Stick your nose right into the bowl and inhale.

Try two or three quick inhalations, or one deep, sharp sniff. The goal is to draw the aromas deep into the nose, where they're registered. It's a remote and protected place, and a head cold or allergies will effectively block it off from even the strongest smells. But with practice, and keen attention, you'll learn how to maximize your perception of aromas, and then how to decipher them.

The world of smell is vast and bewildering. Our olfactory equipment is incredibly sensitive, and our analytic capacity extraordinary: Estimates of the number of different smells humans can identify range up to 10,000.

Serious wine tasters love to identify smells. "Chocolate!" cries one. "Burnt matches!" insists another. "Tea, tobacco and mushrooms," intones a third. Are they just playing word games?

Bill Milne

9

In fact, wine does smell of more than grapes. Chemical analysis has identified the same molecules in wine that give many familiar objects their distinctive scents. Here are just a few: rose, peach, honey and vanilla. Who's to say that some of the more imaginative descriptors—from road tar to smoked bacon—aren't grounded in some basic chemical affinity?

As with color, wine's aromas offer insights into character, origin and history. Some commentators divide the aromatic components into several classes: those produced by the grapes themselves, those introduced by the chemical processes of winemaking and, finally, those that result from the evolution of the wine over time in the bottle. Sometimes the first two classes are called the "aroma," while the third is called the "bouquet."

The biggest impact on a wine's aroma occurs after fermentation, when the wine is held for maturation before bottling. Some wines are simply pumped into large vats, generally made of stainless steel, epoxied concrete or old wood. The large volume of the liquid and the neutral nature of the container do nothing to modify the fruit character inherent in the wine. Other (generally more ambitious and expensive) wines are racked into small (60-gallon) oak barrels. If the barrels are old, they too will be basically neutral, adding little in the way of flavor or aroma. If they are new, however, the wine absorbs elements from the wood that can add aromas (and flavors) of vanilla, smoke, toast, coffee, even chocolate. These aromas will vary in character and intensity depending on whether the oak is French or American in origin, how much the inside of the barrels have been charred, or "toasted," and what percentage of the barrels are new.

Time in the bottle also influences aromas. Young wines smell of fruit; as red wines age, their bouquet evolves into complex, earthy perfumes that mingle cedar, tobacco, tea, mushrooms and spices. Young wines can be delicious, but a great wine aged to perfect maturity is a glorious experience, and once sniffed will never be forgotten.

So when you smell a Cabernet (for example) and find scents that remind you of plums or blackberries, joined by aromas of vanilla and toast, you can reasonably assume the wine is young, made from ripe grapes and aged in a high percentage of new barrels—the "formula" that most often results in concentrated, age-worthy wines. If there are herbal, vegetal or other "green" notes, you may suspect the growing season was cool or short, preventing the grapes from achieving complete maturity. If the fruit smells "cooked," ripe and sweet like jam or even raisins, overripe fruit from a long, hot summer is a likely cause.

Finally, don't simply sniff for clues. Revel in the sensation. Scientists say smells have direct access to the brain, connecting immediately to memory and emotion. Like a lover's perfume, or the scent of cookies from childhood, wine's aromas can evoke a specific place and time with uncanny power.

Tasting Wine

Now comes the best part. Actually drinking the wine is what fulfills its true purpose.

You might think it's the easiest part, too. After all, you learned to drink from a cup when you were two years old, and have been practicing diligently ever since. But there's a huge distinction between swallowing and tasting, the same gulf that yawns between simply hearing and truly listening. Once again, correct technique is essential to full appreciation.

With the aromas still reverberating through your senses, put the glass to your lips and take some liquid in. You need enough to work it all around your mouth, but not so much that you're forced to swallow right away.

Because you don't want to swallow, not just yet. Keep a pleasant wine in your mouth for 10 to 15 seconds, maybe more. Roll it all around, bringing it into contact with every part of your mouth, because each responds to a different aspect of the liquid.

Our taste buds are blunt instruments—most of what we "taste" is actually perceived by our sense of smell—but they do provide basic information, particularly about sweetness and acidity. Just as important are other physical sensations perceived in the mouth, such as a wine's body, astringency and level of alcohol.

Acidity is inherent in the grapes, though in hot climates winemakers may add some tartaric or citric acid to balance the sugar in ultraripe fruit. Acidity can also be manipulated through a process called malolactic fermentation, which is actually a bacterial

Kent Hanson

activity, not a true fermentation. This process takes place after alcoholic fermentation, almost always in red wines and selectively in whites, depending on what the winemaker hopes to achieve. It transforms rather harsh malic acid (the kind found in green apples) to gentler, rounder lactic acid (the kind found in milk)—yielding softer wines that, especially in whites, often show marked buttery or creamy flavors.

Alcohol level—experienced as heat or burning in the back of the throat—results primarily from the ripeness of the grapes at harvest. (Since fermentation is the process of turning sugar into alcohol, more sugar in the grapes equals more strength in the wine.) Most table wines are sold at alcohol levels of 11 to 13 percent. A relatively high alcohol level gives a wine a rich texture and a full body. Alcohol also provides a subliminal sweetness that's necessary to balance the acid and bitter components inevitably present in wine.

A wine's astringency—most perceptible on the taster's inner cheeks—derives from tannins. Tannins are elements extracted primarily from grape skins (and so found mostly in red wines), but they can also come from stems or seeds, and from oak, especially new oak barrels. Young red wines meant for long aging are pumped full of tannins—usually by extending the period that the grape juice spends in contact with the skins—because tannins act as a preservative, and their chemical evolution toward softer, silkier textures is part of the maturation of great wines.

The strength of all of these taste sensations can be amplified through specialized techniques that, frankly, are more appropriate to the tasting lab than the dining room. You might try pursing your lips and inhaling gently through them as you hold the wine in your mouth. This creates a bubbling noise children find immensely amusing; it also accelerates vaporization, intensifying the aromas. Then chew the wine vigorously, sloshing it around in your mouth, to draw out every last nuance of flavor.

After you've sought out all these sensations, you are finally ready to swallow. Don't stop concentrating, though. After you swallow, exhale gently and slowly through both your nose and mouth. (The passage which connects the throat and the nose is another avenue for aromas.)

The finish—the taste that lingers for seconds, even minutes, when the wine is gone—is a good indicator of the wine's ageworthiness and ultimate quality. You'll find that the better the wine, the more complex, profound and long-lasting these residual aromas can be. If the finish is short, the wine is simple and probably meant for early drinking. With great wines, sensitive tasters and minimal distractions, the finish can last a minute or more.

With age, a wine that may be a collection of impressive but disparate impressions in its youth will become more harmonious and complex. One of the most important and least certain judgments a wine taster makes is when a wine will reach its peak, creating a seamless web of color, aroma and flavor. One reason to consider investing in buying a wine by the case is to follow its evolution through the years. This maximizes your chances of catching the wine at its best.

The Language of Wine Tasting

Understanding the wine you taste is only half the battle; communicating your impressions to others in words is just as big a challenge. And since the wine itself disappears as you drink it, verbal descriptions are the only way to preserve the pleasure wine provides.

The goal in tasting wine is not to "find" the same aromas and flavors some other taster is describing. If you hone your own perceptual abilities and develop the vocabulary to articulate them, you'll not only derive more pleasure from the wine itself, but also stimulate better communication between you and the friends who are sharing the bottle.

The best way to develop your own wine vocabulary is to write your own tasting notes. You'll find that certain words recur as descriptors of similar wines, and soon you'll be fluently describing your sensations. The following is a sampling of terms used by professional wine tasters, but again, the bottom line of tasting is your own pleasure; your description should reflect your judgment.

Aggressive: Unpleasantly harsh in taste or texture, usually due to a high level of tannin or acid.

Appearance: Refers to a wine's clarity, not color.

Astringent: Describes a rough, harsh, puckery feel in the mouth, usually from tannin or high acidity, that red wines (and a few whites) have.

Austere: Used to describe relatively hard, high-acid wines that lack depth and roundness. Usually said of young wines that need time to soften, or wines that lack richness and body.

Backbone: Used to denote those wines that are full-bodied, well-structured and balanced by a desirable level of acidity.

Backward: Used to describe a young wine that is less developed than others of its type and class from the same vintage.

Bitter: One source of bitterness in wine is tannin or stems. If the bitter quality dominates the wine's flavor or aftertaste, it is considered a fault.

Blunt: Strong in flavor and often alcoholic, but lacking in aromatic interest and development on the palate.

Body: The impression of weight or fullness on the palate; usually the result of a combination of glycerin, alcohol and sugar.

Bouquet: The smell that a wine develops after it has been bottled and aged. Most appropriate for mature wines that have developed complex flavors beyond basic young fruit and oak aromas.

Brilliant: Describes the appearance of very clear wines with absolutely no visible suspended or particulate matter. Not always a plus, as it can indicate a highly filtered wine.

Browning: Describes a wine's color, and is a sign that a wine is mature and may be faded. A bad sign in young red (or white) wines.

Burnt: Describes wines that have an overdone, smoky, toasty or singed edge. Also used to describe overripe grapes.

Buttery: Indicates the smell of melted butter or toasty oak. Also a reference to texture, as in "a rich, buttery Chardonnay."

Cedary: Denotes the smell of cedar wood associated with mature Cabernet Sauvignon and Cabernet blends aged in French or American oak.

Chewy: Describes rich, heavy, tannic wines that are full-bodied.

Closed: Describes wines that are concentrated and have character, yet are shy in aroma or flavor.

Cloudiness: Lack of clarity to the eye. Fine for old wines with sediment, but it can be a warning signal in younger wines.

Cloying: Describes ultrasweet or sugary wines that lack the balance provided by acid, alcohol, bitterness or intense flavor.

Coarse: Usually refers to texture, and in particular, excessive tannin or oak. Also used to describe harsh bubbles in sparkling wines.

Corked: Describes a wine having the off-putting, musty, moldy-newspaper flavor and aroma and dry aftertaste caused by a tainted cork.

Delicate: Used to describe light-to-medium-weight wines with good flavors. A desirable quality in Pinot Noir or Riesling.

Depth: Describes the complexity and concentration of flavors in a wine, as in "a wine with excellent or uncommon depth."

Dirty: Covers any and all foul, rank, off-putting smells that can occur in a wine, including those caused by bad barrels or corks.

Dry: Having no perceptible taste of sugar.

Drying Out: Losing fruit (or sweetness in sweet wines) to the extent that acid, alcohol or tannin dominate the taste. At this stage the wine will not improve.

Dumb: Describes a phase young wines undergo when their flavors and aromas are undeveloped. A synonym of closed.

Earthy: At its best, a pleasant, clean quality that adds complexity to aroma and flavors. The flip side is a funky, barnyardy character that borders on or crosses into dirtiness.

Elegant: Used to describe wines of grace, balance and beauty.

Fading: Describes a wine that is losing color, fruit or flavor, usually as a result of age.

Fat: Full-bodied, high in alcohol and low in acidity. Can be a plus with bold, ripe, rich flavors.

Finish: Also called aftertaste. Great wines have rich, long, complex finishes.

Flabby: Soft, feeble, lacking acidity on the palate.

Flinty: A descriptor for extremely dry white wines such as Sauvignon Blanc, whose bouquet is reminiscent of flint struck against steel.

Floral (also Flowery): Literally, having the characteristic aroma of flowers. Mostly associated with white wines.

Fresh: Having a lively, clean and fruity character. An essential for young wines.

Grapey: Characterized by simple flavors and aromas associated with fresh table grapes; distinct from the more complex fruit flavors (currant, black cherry, fig or apricot) found in fine wines.

Grassy: A signature descriptor for Sauvignon Blanc, and a pleasant one unless overbearing and pungent.

Green: Tasting of unripe fruit or made from unripe grapes. Can be pleasant in Riesling and Gewürztraminer.

Hard: Firm; a quality that usually results from high acidity or tannins. Often a descriptor for young red wines.

Heady: Used to describe high-alcohol wines.

Hearty: Used to describe the full, warm, sometimes rustic qualities found in red wines with high alcohol.

Herbacious, Herbal: The taste and smell of herbs. A plus in many wines such as Sauvignon Blanc, and to a lesser extent Merlot and Cabernet.

Hollow: Lacking in flavor. Describes a wine that has a first taste and a short finish, and lacks depth at mid-palate.

Hot: High alcohol, unbalanced wines that tend to burn on the finish are called "hot." Acceptable in Port-style wines.

Leafy: Describes a slightly vegetal quality reminiscent of leaves.

Lean: Often a synonym for austere. May indicate a wine lacking in fruit flavors.

Legs: The viscous droplets that form and ease down the sides of the glass when the wine is swirled.

Length: The amount of time the sensations of taste and aroma persist after swallowing. The longer the better.

Maderized: Describes the brownish color and slightly sweet, somewhat caramelized and often nutty character found in mature dessert-style wines.

17

Malic: Describes the green apple-like flavor found in young grapes.

Mature: Ready to drink.

Meaty: Describes red wines that show plenty of concentration and a chewy quality. They may even have an aroma of cooked meat.

Musty: Having an off-putting moldy or mildewy smell. The result of a wine being made from moldy grapes, stored in improperly cleaned tanks and barrels, or contaminated by a poor cork.

Nose: The scent or smell of a wine. Also called aroma; includes bouquet.

Nutty: Used to describe oxidized wines, and thus often indicates a flaw, but when close to an oaky flavor nuttiness can be a plus.

Oaky: Describes the aroma or taste imparted to a wine by the oak barrels or casks in which it was aged. Can be either positive or negative. The terms toasty, vanilla, dill, cedary and smoky indicate the desirable qualities of oak; charred, burnt, green cedar, lumber and plywood describe its unpleasant side.

John Kuczala

Off-dry: Indicates a slightly sweet wine.

Perfumed: Describes the strong, usually sweet and floral aromas of some white wines.

Pruny: Having a prune-like flavor that suggests overripe, dried-out grapes. Can add complexity in the right dose.

Puckery: Describes highly tannic and very dry wines.

Raw: Young and undeveloped. A good descriptor of barrel samples of red wine. Raw wines are often tannic and high in alcohol or acidity.

Residual Sugar: Unfermented grape sugar in a finished wine.

Rich: Wines with generous, full, pleasant flavors are described as rich. In dry wines, richness may be supplied by complex flavors and by an oaky, vanilla character. Sweet wines are also described as rich when they possess fruity, ripe flavors.

Round: Describes a texture that is smooth, not coarse or tannic.

Rustic: Tasting like wines made in an earlier era. Can be a positive quality in distinctive wines that require aging. Can be negative when used to describe a young, earthy wine that should be fresh and fruity.

Soft: Describes wines low in acid or tannin (sometimes both), making for easy drinking. Opposite of hard.

Spicy: Denotes the presence of spice flavors—such as anise, cinnamon, cloves, mint and pepper—which are often present in complex wines.

Stemmy, Stalky: Describes an unpleasant, often dominant, green, astringent aroma and flavor. Develops when wines are fermented too long with the grape stems.

Structure: The interaction of elements such as acid, tannin, glycerin, alcohol and body as it relates to a wine's texture and mouthfeel. Usually preceded by a modifier, as in "firm structure" or "lacking in structure."

John Kuczala

Tannin: The mouth-puckering substance—found mostly in red wines—that is derived primarily from grape skins, seeds and stems, but also from oak barrels. Tannin acts as a natural preservative that helps wine age and develop.

Tight: Describes a wine's structure, concentration and body, as in a "tightly wound" wine. Closed and compact are similar terms.

Tinny: Metallic tasting.

Toasty: A flavor derived from the oak barrels in which wines are aged. Also sometimes develops in sparkling wines.

Vegetal: Containing aromas or flavors which are reminiscent of plants and vegetables. Usually considered a flaw.

Velvety: Having rich flavor and a silky, sumptuous texture.

Getting the Most from Wine

Enjoying a wine's flavor to the fullest depends primarily on the concentration and perceptual ability of the taster. But the right tools and an efficient approach can make a big difference, too.

Technical details include the serving temperature of the wine, proper opening and pouring methods, the decision whether or not to decant the bottle and appropriate stemware.

The "correct" temperature, like so many details in wine tasting, is ultimately a matter of personal preference. But wine temperature influences wine flavor, and there are good reasons to follow time-tested practices.

Cold temperatures enhance the perception of bitterness; warm ones increase the impact of sweetness and alcohol. According to French enologist Emile Peynaud, "the same red wine will seem thin and hot at 72°F, supple and fluid at 64°F, full and astringent at 50°F." So a powerful, tannic red should be poured warm enough to minimize its astringency, but not so warm as to emphasize its alcohol. We drink sweet white wines well chilled to keep their sweetness in balance.

We recommend serving:
- full-bodied and mature red wines at 60°F to 65°F
- light-bodied young reds at 55°F to 60°F
- dry whites at 45°F to 50°F
- sweet whites at 40°F to 50°F.

Remember that the wine will warm up in the glass, since most dining rooms are heated to 70°F or more, so it's better to serve them a couple of degrees too cold than too warm.

The way you open the bottle won't normally affect its flavors, but as part of the ceremony of wine it helps put the tasters in a receptive mood. If a capsule covers the neck of the bottle, cut it cleanly below the protruding lip and remove the top portion (or simply take the whole thing off). Wipe the neck of the bottle to remove any mold or mineral salts that may have accumulated. Using a corkscrew that feels comfortable in your hand (we prefer the screwpull, or a simple waiter's corkscrew, as shown at far left), pull the cork slowly, trying not to disturb any sediment in the wine, and clean the inside of the bottle neck before pouring.

Should you decant the wine—that is, pour it from the bottle into a different container for serving? Yes, if the wine has thrown a heavy deposit; vintage Port and full-bodied, mature reds are the usual culprits here. (But decanting is useless if the sediment is floating throughout the wine; be sure to stand the bottle upright for a day or two before opening.) Yes, if you want to show off an heirloom crystal decanter or hide the identity of the wine. In all other cases, decanting is useless at best, harmful at worst.

Bill Milne

This advice flouts some conventional wisdom, which argues that young reds (and occasionally other wines as well) benefit from "breathing" and need the vigorous contact with oxygen that decanting provides in order to "open up" and show their best. No scientific evidence supports this point of view. It is true that wines change with exposure to air, but mostly for the worse—old wines, for example, may deteriorate rapidly after opening. Instead of decanting, try following the arc of a wine's evolution right in the glass, from the first taste until the last sip (which may come hours later).

Don't forget the glasses. Any container that will hold water can serve wine, but appropriate stemware not only adds beauty to the table, it also enhances the wine's taste. Austrian glassmaker Georg Riedel sells special glasses specifically made for dozens of particular wine types, and other stemware makers offer five or six different types (red, white, Champagne, Sherry, Port, etc.). If cost is no object, it pays to tailor your stemware to your wines. On the other hand, there is such a thing as a perfectly acceptable "all-purpose" wine glass.

In our experience, the best wine glass is a slender goblet of thin, clear crystal with a long stem on a sturdy base. (Heavy cut glass may take light beautifully, but it blunts the contact between wine and tongue, and examining wine through colored glass is like gazing at a beautiful friend who's wearing wraparound sunglasses.) The glass should hold 10 to 18 ounces—but never be filled more than half full, so there's enough air space to release the wine's aromas. The bowl should be biggest at the bottom, tapering to a smaller opening, in order to concentrate those aromas.

Finally, there's the matter of storage. If you plan to buy wine one to a few bottles at a time, and consume

it within a month or two, a small rack away from any direct heat source is all that's necessary. Do keep the bottles on their sides, so the corks don't dry out and permit air to enter. And remember that temperatures greater than 70 degrees Fahrenheit may age a wine too quickly, and can even "cook" it until the fruit flavors and aromas become blunted.

If at some point you decide to collect fine wines that will benefit from additional bottle aging, you will need a cool space with constant temperature for long-term storage. If you have a naturally cool space such as a below-ground basement, that's fine; if not, you may wish to invest in a temperature-controlled storage unit.

Wine Buying Strategies

Jon Wyand

Regardless of your level of interest in wine, you're in for both fun and a challenge when you decide to buy wine purposefully. Wine is a living thing and is constantly changing. Every year you'll be presented with a seemingly endless stream of new wines, producers, appellations and vintages. Even if you find a winery or style of wine that appeals to you now, your taste will likely change over time and you'll discover new horizons. The combination of possibilities is endless.

Devising a buying strategy can be as simple as choosing a few brands you like and sticking with them. This is a tried-and-true way to keep a cellar stocked with reliable wines that suit your taste and budget.

More daring collectors expand their hobby of wine collecting into a more sophisticated enterprise. They may collect verticals (different vintages from the same producer) of the world's greatest wines, or they may buy wine futures—paying in advance (before the vintage is released) for one or more cases of wine from a top producer, in order to lock in a price they expect will rise after release.

Rule No. 1 of buying wine is to trust your own taste. No one knows your taste preferences better than you, so it's important to be comfortable deciding which wines appeal to you and which don't. You'll be far happier with your buying decisions if you taste a wine and decide you like it before committing to more bottles. Even if your friends or wine critics rave about a wine, there's no guarantee that you'll like it.

Gaining experience with the world's fine wines takes time, but it is a fascinating journey. You're likely to learn as much from your buying mistakes as you will from your triumphs. Part of the fun of wine is learning where and how it's grown and vinified, which food types match well with different wines, and which wine types and vintages improve with cellaring and bottle age.

Before you start buying wine, it's a good idea to assess your needs. How much wine do you drink and on what occasions? Do you want to cellar young wines for drinking in a few years? You may also decide to budget money for your wine hobby so you can determine how much you can realistically afford to spend on wine.

It's easy to buy more wine than you genuinely need. Buying wine on a whim can be fun, particularly when you spot a special bottle you've been looking for. But fanciful buying also increases the odds that you'll end up with a wine you may not need for which you may have paid too much. Planning ahead allows you to set aside a specific amount of money for buying wine by the case. Many retailers and wineries offer a 10 percent discount for case purchases. Discount stores, however, usually pass along the 10 percent discount on all purchases.

Once you've outlined your needs, you'll need a place to shop. Years ago, about the only source to buy fine wine was the traditional fine-wine merchant. Today your options abound. In some states, you'll see fine wine in scores of discount chain stores and upscale supermarkets, some of which present a dazzling selection. Retailers have also become more aggressively promotional, announcing sales in newspaper and magazine ads and selling wine via toll-free telephone numbers and the internet. A growing list of retailers publish catalogs, especially during the holiday season, offering hundreds of wines and special gift packages. There are even wine-of-the-month clubs. Once you join, the club selects wines for you and ships them to your home for you to sample. Some wineries in the United States will ship wines directly to the customers on their mailing list, but the legality of such purchases varies by state. Most of the

James Baigrie

time, though, you'll be purchasing wine at a retail store, so it helps to get to know your local wine stores and merchants, including what kinds of wines they stock and their pricing strategies.

A well-informed retailer is an excellent source of sound buying advice and tips about what's new and interesting in his store. Retailers can also help find special wines that may be hard to locate. Some retail stores even do the shopping for their customers. When a special wine comes in, they set aside a few bottles or a case and bill the customer, holding the wine until it's picked up.

While you're visiting wine shops, take special notice of how the wines are stored and if the temperature is cool. Light and heat are enemies of wine. Wine shops that are hot in the summer are probably not the best place to buy your wines. It's also wise to examine the bottles you're planning to buy to make sure the fill level is good—up to the neck of the bottle—and that wine hasn't leaked through the cork. If wine leaks out, that means air is getting into the bottle and oxidizing the wine. Avoid bottles with low fills or leaks.

One fun way to defray the cost of tasting a broad selection of wines is to join a club or group that tastes wines regularly. This way you can afford to taste expensive wines such as Château Lafite Rothschild, Romanée-Conti, Gaja or Château d'Yquem. Each member brings a bottle of wine to the tasting and shares it among six, eight or 12 people. Some wine syndicates even order cases of wines together, which is another way to cut costs (with a 10 percent discount) and broaden your exposure to the world of fine wines.

When you're on the road touring wine country, you'll also discover that many wineries have specialty wines or older vintages no longer on the market that they sell only at the winery. Be on the lookout for some of those rarities, but don't necessarily expect to find great bargains. Most wineries sell their wines on-site at full retail price. You can often find the same bottles for less at your local retail outlet.

Bill Milne

Judging a Wine by Its Label

More people choose wines by their labels than are comfortable admitting it. Novices reach for pretty pictures; snobs demand famous names. But in fact, a wine label reveals a great deal about the flavors in the bottle. You can begin your tasting even before you've pulled the cork.

Although each country differs on what information is required by law to be included on a wine label, every label gives some clues to the wine inside the bottle. For example, the producer's name is always prominent. Most wineries develop consistent taste profiles, based on their location, winemaking skills and marketing goals; once you're familiar with a winery's profile, the producer's name is perhaps the most reliable indicator of wine style and quality.

The wine's vintage is almost always shown, too. If you're familiar with the vintages of a given region, this can be a telling indicator—red Bordeaux wines were mostly light and diluted in 1992, but opulent and harmonious in 1995. (We've included a handy pull-out vintage chart in the back of this book to help.) However, even if you don't know whether a specific vintage was good or bad, knowing how old a wine is indicates something about its current style: young, fresh and fruity, or older, smoother and more complex. Most whites, and very many reds, are best within three years of the vintage; wines that age well increase in price over time. Beware of old, inexpensive wines.

Finally, don't forget the price tag, stuck right there next to the label. Yes, there may be wide disparities between a wine's cost and its quality.

If you're spending under $6 per bottle, the wine is likely to be simple, offering alcohol as its principal virtue. From $6 to $12, most wines offer fresh fruit, enough structure to marry well with food and some individual personality. From $12 to, say, $50 and upwards, you can expect complex flavors of ripe fruit and new oak, enough concentration to develop with aging and a distinctive character stamped with the wine's creator and origin. Pay any more, and you enter into a rarefied world inhabited by passionate and deep-pocketed collectors; the rest of us usually pass by with a shake of the head.

Wineries put a lot of effort into their labels. Savvy wine lovers can decipher what the law says they must say, what the producers want to say—and sometimes more than they intend to say. Spend some time studying labels before you buy and you'll increase your chances of finding a wine to suit your tastes.

Varietal Characteristics

I n order to appreciate wine, it's essential to under-
stand the characteristics different grapes offer and
how those characteristics should be expressed in
wines. Cabernet Sauvignon, Merlot and Zinfandel are
all red grapes, but as wines their personalities are
quite different. Even when grown in different appellations and vinified using different techniques, a varietal
wine always displays certain qualities that are inherent in the grape's personality. Understanding what a
grape should be as a wine is fundamental, and knowing what a grape can achieve at its greatest is the
essence of fine-wine appreciation.

Barbera (Red) [bar-BEHR-uh]: Its wines are characterized by a high level of acidity (meaning brightness and
crispness), deep ruby color and full body, with low tannin levels; flavors are berrylike. Most successful in
Italy's Piedmont region.

Brunello (Red) [broo-NEHL-oh]: This strain of Sangiovese is
the only grape permitted for Brunello di Montalcino, the
rare, costly Tuscan red that at its best is loaded with lus-
cious black and red fruits and chewy tannins.

Cabernet Franc (Red) [cab-er-NAY FRAHNK]: Increasingly
popular as both a stand-alone varietal and blending
grape. Typically light- to medium-bodied wine with
more immediate fruit than Cabernet Sauvignon and
some of the herbaceous odors evident in unripe
Cabernet Sauvignon.

Cabernet Sauvignon (Red) [cab-er-NAY SO-vin-yon]: The
undisputed king of red wines, Cabernet is a remarkably
steady and consistent performer. In specific appellations
it is capable of rendering wines of uncommon depth,
richness, concentration and longevity. Its classic flavors
are currant, plum, black cherry and spice. It can also be
marked by herb, olive, mint, tobacco, cedar, anise, and
ripe, jammy notes. The best Cabernets start out dark
purple-ruby in color, with firm acidity, a full body, great
intensity, concentrated flavors and firm tannins.

Carignan (Red) [kar-in-YAHN]: Also known as Carignane (California), Cirnano (Italy). Once a major blending grape for jug wines, Carignan's popularity has diminished.

Chardonnay (White) [SHAR-dun-NAY]: As Cabernet Sauvignon is the king of reds, so is Chardonnay the king of white wines, for it makes consistently excellent, rich and complex whites. This is an amazingly versatile grape that grows well in a variety of locations throughout the world. When well made, Chardonnay offers bold, ripe, rich and intense fruit flavors of apple, fig, melon, pear, peach, pineapple, lemon and grapefruit, along with spice, honey, butter, butterscotch and hazelnut flavors.

Chardonnay
David Prince

Chenin Blanc (White) [SHEN'n BLAHNK]: This native of the Loire Valley in France has two personalities: at home it's the basis of such famous, long-lived whites as Vouvray and Saumer, but on other soils—especially South Africa (where it is called Steen) and California—it is primarily a very good blending grape. It can yield a pleasant enough wine on its own, with subtle melon, peach, spice and citrus notes.

Dolcetto (Red) [dole-CHET-to]: Almost exclusive to Italy's northwest Piedmont region, this varietal produces soft, round, fruity wines, fragrant with licorice and almonds, that should be drunk within about three years after bottling.

French Colombard (White) [kahl-um-BARRED]: The king of white jug-wine grapes. Virtually all of it goes into inexpensive jug wines. It makes clean and simple wines with firm acidity.

Fumé Blanc (White) [FOO-may BLAHNK]: see Sauvignon Blanc.

Gamay (Red) [ga-MAY]: Beaujolais makes its famous, fruity reds exclusively from one of the many Gamays available, the Gamay Noir à Jus Blanc. Low in alcohol and relatively high in acidity, the wines are meant to be drunk soon after bottling; the ultimate example of this is Beaujolais Nouveau, whipped onto shelves everywhere almost overnight.

Gewürztraminer

David Prince

Gewürztraminer (White) [geh-VERTS-trah-mee-ner]: Gewürztraminer can yield magnificent wines, as is best demonstrated in Alsace, France, where it is made in to a variety of styles from dry to off-dry to sweet. At its best, it produces a floral and refreshing wine with crisp acidity that pairs well with spicy dishes. When fully ripe grapes are left on the vine for late harvest, they can yield a tremendous, uncommonly rich and complex dessert wine.

Grenache (Red) [greh-NAHSH]: Drought- and heat-resistant, it yields a fruity, spicy, medium-bodied wine with supple tannins. The second most widely planted grape in the world, Grenache—although also bottled alone—is a very popular blending grape.

Malbec (Red) [MAHL-beck]: Once important in Bordeaux and the Loire in various blends, this not-very-hardy grape has been steadily replaced by Merlot and the two Cabernets. However, Argentina is markedly successful with this varietal.

Marsanne (White) [mahr-SANN]: At its best, Marsanne can be a full-bodied, moderately intense wine with spice, pear and citrus notes. Popular in the Rhône region of France (along with Grenache Blanc, Roussanne and Viognier). Australia, especially Victoria, has some of the world's oldest vineyards.

Merlot (Red) [mur-LO]: Once used mainly in the Bordeaux blend, Merlot can stand alone as a varietal wine, and has recently become quite fashionable. Despite its popularity, its quality ranges only from good to very good most of the time, though there are a few stellar producers found around the world. Several styles have emerged. One is a blend which includes a notable percentage of Cabernet, and contains similar currant and cherry flavors and firm tannins. A second style is less reliant on Cabernet, softer, more supple, less tannic, medium in weight, and features more herb and chocolate flavors. A third style is a very light and simple wine; this type's sales are fueling Merlot's overall growth. Merlot's aging potential is fair to good. It may become softer with age, but often the fruit flavors fade and the herbal flavors dominate.

Mourvèdre (Red) [more-VAY-druh]: As long as the weather is warm, Mourvèdre likes a wide variety of soils. It's popular across the south of France, and Spain uses it in many areas. The wine can be pleasing, with medium-weight, spicy cherry and berry flavors and moderate tannins. It ages well.

Muscat (White) [MUSS-kat]: Known as Muscat, Muscat Blanc and Muscat Canelli, it is marked by strong spice and floral notes and can be used in blending or made into a dessert (sweet) wine.

Nebbiolo (Red) [NEH-bee-oh-low]: The great grape of Northern Italy, which excels there in Barolo and Barbaresco, both strong, ageable wines. Mainly unsuccessful elsewhere, Nebbiolo also now has a small foothold in California. So far the California wines are light and uncomplicated, bearing no resemblance to the Italian types.

Petite Sirah (Red) [peh-TEET sih-RAH]: Long favored as a blending grape in France and California, giving otherwise simple, light-colored wines more color, depth, intensity and tannin. It is probably not related to Syrah.

Pinot Blanc (White) [PEE-no BLAHNK]: Often referred to as a poor man's Chardonnay because of its similar flavor and texture profile, Pinot Blanc is used in Champagne, Burgundy, Alsace, Germany, Italy and California and can make a terrific wine. When well made, it is intense, concentrated and complex, with ripe pear, spice, citrus and honey notes. Can age, but is best early on while its fruit shines through.

Pinot Gris or Pinot Grigio (White) [PEE-no GREE or GREE-zho]: Known as Pinot Grigio in Italy, where it is mainly found in the northeast, producing quite a lot of undistinguished dry white wine and Collio's excellent whites. As Pinot Gris, it used to be grown in Burgundy and the Loire, but it has been supplanted there; it comes into its own in Alsace, where it's known as Tokay (no relation to the Hungarian Tokay dessert wine). Southern Germany plants it as Ruländer. When good, this varietal is soft, gently perfumed, and has more color than most whites.

Pinot Gris

David Prince

Pinot Noir (Red) [PEE-no NWAHR]: Pinot Noir, the great grape of Burgundy, is a touchy variety. The best examples offer the classic black cherry, spice, raspberry and currant flavors, and an aroma that can resemble wilted roses, along with earth, tar, herb and cola notes. It can also be rather ordinary, light, simple, herbal, vegetal and occasionally weedy. It can even be downright funky, with pungent barnyard aromas. In fact, Pinot Noir is the most fickle of all grapes.

Riesling (White) [REES-ling]: Rieslings share a distinctive floral bouquet, but beyond that they vary widely. In Germany's Mosel-Saar-Ruwer area, the wines are delicate and subtle, with very low alcohol; in the Pfalz they become spicy, exuberant and full-bodied; in Alsace they are bone-dry. Grows best in cool areas that allow the grapes to ripen slowly, so it is also found in Canada—where it sometimes yields eiswein (ice wine), an intensely flavored dessert wine made from grapes touched by frost—and in Oregon, Washington and New York states.

Sangiovese (Red) [san-joe-VEHS-eh]: Sangiovese is the backbone of many superb Italian red wines, from Chianti to Brunello di Montalcino. It's distinctive for its supple texture and medium- to full-bodied spice, raspberry, cherry and anise flavors. When blended with a grape such as Cabernet Sauvignon, Sangiovese gives the resulting wine a smoother texture and lightens up the tannins.

Sauvignon Blanc
David Prince

Sauvignon Blanc (White) [SO-vin-yon BLAHNK]: Another white with a notable aroma, often described as "grassy;" the flavor profile often includes green apple or citrus fruits. Generally tastes best when young and fresh. Sauvignon Blanc grows well in many areas of the world. It mixes well with Sémillon, and many vintners add a touch of Chardonnay for extra body. As a late-harvest sweet wine, it's often fantastic, capable of yielding amazingly complex and rich flavors.

Sémillon (White) [SEM-ih-yon]: On its own or in a blend, this is one of the few whites that can age. It can make a wonderful late-harvest dessert wine, with complex fig, pear, tobacco and honey notes. When paired with its traditional partner, Sauvignon Blanc, it adds body, flavor and texture, yielding a satisfying table wine. It can also be found blended with Chardonnay, more to add volume than to add anything to the flavor profile.

Syrah or Shiraz (Red) [sih-RAH or shih-RAHZ]: The epitome of Syrah is a majestic wine that can age for half a century, the best of which come from Hermitage and Côte-Rôtie in France and Penfolds Grange in Australia. The grape seems to grow well in a number of areas and is capable of rendering rich, complex and distinctive wines, with pronounced pepper, spice, black cherry, tar, leather and roasted nut flavors, a smooth, supple texture and smooth tannins.

Trebbiano or Ugni Blanc (White) [treh-bee-AH-no or OO-nee BLAHNK]: This grape is called Trebbiano in Italy and Ugni Blanc in France. It is tremendously prolific; low in alcohol but high in acidity, it is found in almost any basic white Italian wine.

Viognier (White) [vee-oh-NYAY]: Viognier, the rare white grape of France's Rhône Valley, is one of the most difficult grapes to grow. But fans of the floral, spicy white wine are thrilled by its prospects in the south of France and the New World.

Viognier
David Prince

Zinfandel (Red) [ZIHN-fan-dell]: The most widely planted red grape in California. Much of it is vinified into white Zinfandel, a blush-colored, slightly sweet wine. Real Zinfandel, the red wine, is the quintessential California wine. It has been used for blending with other grapes, including Cabernet Sauvignon and Petite Sirah. It has been made in a claret style, with berry and cherry flavors, mild tannins and pretty oak shadings. It has been made into a full-bodied, ultraripe, intensely flavored and firmly tannic wine designed to age. And it has been made into late-harvest and Port-style wines that feature very ripe, raisiny flavors, alcohol above 15 percent and chewy tannins. Recent styles, aiming for the mainstream rather than the extreme, emphasize the grape's zesty, spicy pepper, raspberry, cherry, wild berry and plum flavors, and its complex range of tar, earth and leather notes.

Where Wine Comes From

Australia

With more than 1000 wineries in production, Australia has become a formidable source of quality wine. Australia made its reputation on a flood of good-value wines, especially Chardonnay that cost less than $10. Today, almost every major grape variety is cultivated here—though there is an increasing

Cabernet Sauvignon vines on red soil in vineyard of Tyrrells. Lower Hunter Valley, New South Wales, Australia.

concentration on a few major red and white varietals—and Australia's best wines compete with the elite of Bordeaux, Burgundy and California in price as well as quality.

Australia, like America, labels its best wines with varietal names. The rules are similar, in that varietal wines are made entirely or mostly from the single grape variety named on the front label. Often more than one variety is named, by order of amount: Shiraz-Cabernet has more Shiraz in it and Cabernet-Shiraz has more Cabernet.

Grape Varieties

The flavors of Australian wines tend to be full and hearty, similar in style to California's. Cabernet Sauvignon and Chardonnay are extremely successful here, as is the more traditional Shiraz (known as Syrah elsewhere). Sémillon, often blended with Chardonnay or Sauvignon Blanc, is worth trying, as are the few Australian Rieslings that make it across the Pacific. Finally, Australia makes some superb dessert wines, including Port-style wines that are comparable to their Portuguese prototypes, and sweet Muscats and Tokays which are among the most complex and distinctive wines in the world.

Wine Regions

Australia's chief wine regions are South Australia (centered around Adelaide), which produces perhaps 60% of the country's wine and includes the respected Barossa Valley and Coonawarra appellations; New South Wales, which extends north of Sydney and encompasses the well-known Hunter Valley; and Victoria, whose Yarra Valley district lies immediately northeast of Melbourne. Often wines from all three regions are blended and sold under the catch-all Southeastern Australia denomination. The only other significant wine region is Western Australia, located south of Perth on the West Coast. Though its wine quality is high, Western Australia accounts for a relatively small percentage of total production.

Chile

Chilean viticulture dates back to the Spanish settlers of the 1550s, who brought the first European vinifera vines. Cuttings of native French grape types—Cabernet Sauvignon, Malbec, Merlot, Sémillon and Sauvignon Blanc—were first imported in the 1850s. The French winemaking tradition remains strong here; Chilean wines still tend more toward the elegant European style than they do toward the heavier, more concentrated style found in much of the rest of the New World (though this is partly attributable to the light Chilean soil).

For many years the Chilean wine industry was

held back by a lack of capital and foreign investment. However, the situation changed dramatically in the mid-1980s, when Chile began to aggressively develop wine as a source of export income.

Much like North American wines, Chilean wines are marketed primarily by varietal labeling (for instance, "Chardonnay") rather than by regional appellations (such as "Maipo Valley").

Grape Varieties

Among red wines Cabernet Sauvignon is the most widely planted, and Merlot production is becoming increasingly significant. Most Chilean wineries also produce decent, sometimes delicious white wines among which Sauvignon Blanc remains the most consistent of the white varieties. Chardonnay is also becoming important; however, generally warm conditions in many regions have meant that Chilean Chardonnays often lack crispness and definition.

Wine Regions

Located in the northern part of Chile's central valley, a narrow, 300-mile long valley set between the Andes and a coastal range of mountains to the west, is the Maipo Valley—the heart of the Chilean wine industry. Farther south, in the Rapel and Maule regions of the valley, a number of newer sub-regions have developed, including Lontue, Colchagua, Curicó and Rancagua. Many producers blend wines from a number of these regions, with the object of producing well balanced reds and whites that combine the flavors of several regions.

France

To know great wine is to know France. No other country offers such a mind-boggling array of fabulous wines—yet much of the 660 million cases of wine made by the thousands of French wine producers each year is very ordinary. France has dozens of different winemaking regions, encompassing every terrain and climate imaginable, from cool mountainsides to desert plains. Furthermore, unlike the United States and many other wine-producing countries,

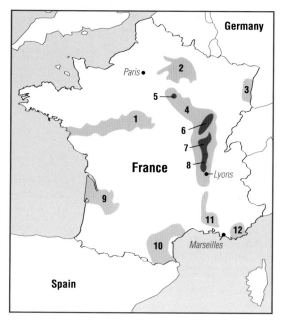

1. Loire	5. Chablis	9. Bordeaux
2. Champagne	6. Côte d'Or	10. Languedoc-Roussillon (d'Oc)
3. Alsace	7. Mâcon	11. Rhône
4. Burgundy	8. Beaujolais	12. Provence

France labels most of its wines according to their origin—region and producer—instead of grape variety. (For instance, Château Pétrus, the famous Pomerol, is made almost entirely of Merlot, but there's no mention of Merlot on the bottle.) Finding your way through this maze can be a challenge, but a very rewarding one.

The French Appellation System

France's *Appellation d'Origine Contrôlée AOC* laws reflect the philosophical underpinning of French winemaking: that the character and quality of a wine derive from the precise interplay of soil, climate, grape variety and the winemaker's skill. There are roughly 250 recognized AC wine types arranged in pyramidal fashion, with large regional appellations, such as Bordeaux, at the base of the pyramid, and single estates at the top. As a (very) general rule, the more tightly specified the AC, the better the

quality of the soil, and the more restrictive the regulations regarding yield per acre, alcoholic content, and
so forth—and thus the better the wine that comes
from that AC.

Bordeaux

The most important region within Bordeaux is the
Médoc, and specifically the Haut-Médoc appellation;
this in turn includes the four villages (or "communes")—Margaux, St.-Julien, Pauillac, and St.-
Estèphe—which produce some of the world's best,
most famous and most expensive red wines (Lafite-
Rothschild and Latour, for example). Cabernet
Sauvignon is the dominant grape here, but it is nearly always blended with some combination of Merlot,
Cabernet Franc, Petit Verdot and Malbec. Merlot
takes the lead role in two other prominent red-wine
communes—Pomerol and St.-Emilion—which lie
west of the Médoc, across the Dordogne River.

South of the Médoc is the Graves region, unusual
for this area in that its white wines are equal in importance to its reds. Sémillon and Sauvignon Blanc are
the main white grapes used. Within Graves lies the
commune of Sauternes, renowned for intensely flavored sweet wines made from Sémillon grapes affected by the "noble rot" mold; Château d'Yquem is its
most famous producer.

Burgundy

Burgundy vineyards are classifed according to quality in a complicated hierarchy ranging from grand
cru at the top to cru bourgeois at the bottom. Most
great vineyards have more than one owner, and the
quality of wine produced from a single vineyard can
vary widely according to the skill of the vintner.
Overall though, fine red and white Burgundies are
extraordinarily complex, and are among the most
avidly sought-after by collectors—in part because
most of them are produced in very small quantities.
Burgundies from less distinguished vineyards are
often bought in bulk and blended by merchant-pro-
ducers called *négociants*, whose goal is a consistent
style from year to year.

The heart of Burgundy is the Côte d'Or. Its northern

half, the Côte de Nuits, specializes in red wine made entirely from the Pinot Noir grape; the southern half, the Côte de Beaune, produces both reds and whites, the latter made almost exclusively from Chardonnay. Other winegrowing portions of Burgundy include Chablis, in the north, whose grand crus are among the world's finest Chardonnays; the Mâconnais, which produces both undistinguished reds and good Chardonnays, such as Pouilly-Fuissé; and Beaujolais, source of the popular, inexpensive, early-drinking red wine, which is made from the Gamay grape.

Champagne

The term Champagne properly refers only to the sparkling wine produced in the Champagne district of France, about 90 miles east of Paris. It also implies a particular procedure, the *méthode champenoise*: after grape juice is fermented into wine in large vats (as in any winemaking process), sugar is added to the liquid, which is then bottled and tightly sealed; the trapped carbon dioxide gas produced by a second fermentation in the bottle is the source of those tiny, delightful bubbles.

Jon Wyand

Vineyards at Le Mesnil-sur-Oger in Champagne.

Most Champagne is a blend of Pinot Noir, Pinot Meunier (both red grapes from which the skins are quickly removed after crushing to prevent coloring the wine), and Chardonnay; when only the last is used, the wine is called *blanc de blancs*. Taste designations found on the label include "extra dry," which, confusingly, means slightly sweet; very dry Champagne is termed "brut." Most Champagne is a blend of vintages, which helps ensure a consistent style, but in exceptional years producers may bottle a vintage-dated product, which tastes distinctive and commands a premium price.

Other Regions

The Loire Valley, in northwestern France, is known for its crisp, dry white wines, which include Sancerre, Pouilly-Fumé (both made from Sauvignon Blanc), and Muscadet; Vouvray, made from Chenin Blanc, can be either dry or sweet. Alsace, on the German border in the northeast, is also predominantly a white-wine area, specializing in the German varietals Riesling and Gewürztraminer, plus Pinot Gris and Pinot Blanc. (It is also the only top-quality French region to systematically label its wines by grape type.) Unlike the German versions of these varietals, Alsatian wines are usually dry, except for those labeled *vendange tardive* (late harvest).

The Rhône valley in the south—Côtes-du-Rhône is the most general appellation used—is best known for its reds, though some whites are made as well. Northern Rhône reds rely mainly on Syrah grapes and whites are either Viognier or Roussanne; major appellations include Côte Rôtie, Hermitage, Cornas and Condrieu. The Southern Rhône is home to Châteauneuf-du-Pape, famous for dark, tannic, intense red wines blended from as many as 13 grape types, including Grenache, Mourvèdre, Cinsault, Syrah and Counoise.

In other parts of France—particularly the Midi, a vast southern wine-producing area that encompasses Languedoc-Roussillon and Provence among other regions—there's been a recent trend toward making and marketing single varietal wines, especially the internationally popular Cabernet Sauvignon, Merlot and Chardonnay. Wines labeled primarily with their grape variety generally carry the additional designation *vin de pays*, which loosely translates as "country wine."

Germany

In marked contrast to their tongue-twisting names and complicated official nomenclature, the sensory appeal of German wines is instantaneous. Good-quality German wines—mostly white—combine abundant fruit with lively, refreshing crispness. Finding a reliable producer whose style appeals to your taste is the key to choosing German wines.

The German Classification System

German wines are categorized according to the ripeness of the grapes at picking, which influences the richness of the resulting wine. (Although they may contain residual sugar, German wines are balanced by high acidity, so they do not necessarily taste sweet.) The minimum levels of ripeness for each category vary by region, but the basic categories are Tafelwein (table wine), Qualitätswein (quality wine or QbA) and Qualitätswein mit Prädikat (quality wine with added distinction or QmP).

Within the latter category the distinctions are (in ascending order of ripeness) Kabinett, Spätlese, Auslese, Beerenauslese and Trockenbeerenauslese (TBA). Kabinett and Spätlese are the German wines that are most similar to fine white table wines produced elsewhere, though they maintain their own distinctiveness. Spätlese can be particularly successful

CEPHAS/Nigel Blythe

View from the Steffensberg vineyard at Kröv, with Wolf on the far bank of the Mosel, Germany.

when made in the very dry "trocken" style or the slightly less dry "halbtrocken" style.

Above this level, the wines are almost always sweet. Auslese is made from select bunches of late harvest grapes. Beerenauslese and Trockenbeerenauslese, intensely flavored dessert wines, are made from individually chosen grapes affected by "noble rot." These two types rank among the greatest sweet wines in the world, and can age for decades.

Grape Varieties and Wine Regions

Riesling is the most important German grape variety and produces the country's greatest wines. (Müller-Thurgau is the most widely planted, and is the chief ingredient in cheap white wines such as Liebfraumilch.) Other very good, even great wines are made from the Gewürztraminer, Scheurebe and Sylvaner grapes.

The unique conditions of soil and climate among Germany's 13 wine-growing regions (including two in the former East German Republic) produce distinctive styles from these grapes. The most important regions are all in the west-central portion of the country. Mosel-Saar-Ruwer wines tend to be the most delicate. Rheinhessen wines are rounder and fruitier, while Nahe wines fall somewhere between the two. Rheingau produces powerful, firmly structured, spicy wines. And the richest, fullest versions of white German wines come from the Pfalz.

Italy

Italy makes more wine than any other country. For many years too many cheap and rustic bottlings kept the country from achieving its potential. But today Italy is rapidly improving the quality of its winemaking, and its reputation rests not on quantity but on quality.

The Italian Appellation System; Grape Varieties

Italy's appellation system is far more complex than that of the United States or France. It has an older system of DOCs *(denominazioni di origine controllata)*, over which was superimposed a newer system of

1. **Piedmont:** Barbera, Dolcetto
2. **Veneto:** Bardolino, Soave, Valpolicella
3. **Trentino-Alto Adige**
4. **Friuli-Venezia**
5. **Tuscany:** Chianti
6. **Umbria:** Orvieto
7. **The Marches:** Verdicchio
8. **Abruzzo:** Montepulciano d'Abruzzo
9. **Apulia**

DOCG (the G stands for *Garantita*, and theoretically indicates a superior standard of wine quality). The 250-plus DOC and DOCG wines must adhere to strict rules about grape types, aging methods, and so forth—all of which inhibit experiment by creative winemakers. The result has been a plethora of *vini da tavola*, so-called "table wines" that are in some cases superior to their DOC and DOCG brethren.

A new category called IGT was established in 1992 in an attempt to bring some order to the chaos. Meanwhile, grape varieties are increasingly getting top billing on wine labels in Italy, as they are on French vin de pays. The leading types include the indigenous Nebbiolo, Sangiovese, Barbera and Dolcetto for reds, and Trebbiano and Pinot Grigio for whites, as well as the internationally ubiquitous Merlot and Chardonnay.

Tuscany

At the heart of Tuscany, in terms of both geography and importance, is the Chianti zone. Although Chianti is blended from several grapes, at its core is the remarkably adaptable Sangiovese, which can yield wines ranging from soft and fruity to deeply colored and tannic. Chianti Classico, which can only come from the strictly defined Classico zone, is the most structured and ageworthy Chianti; the Riserva designation is reserved for its best wines. On a level with Chianti Classico is the much smaller Chianti Rufina zone, in the hills east of Florence. Nearby is the area

The Tuscan vineyards of Altesino produce top Brunello di Montalcino.

called Pomino, which produces reds made from Cabernet, Sangiovese and Merlot, and some excellent Chardonnay-based whites.

In southern Tuscany is found the austerely powerful Brunello di Montalcino, which along with Barolo is Italy's most acclaimed—and often its most expensive—traditional red wine. The only permissible grape for this DOCG is the Sangiovese Grosso, a potent clone of the Sangiovese. East of Montalcino, Vino Nobile di Montepulciano, also made from a local clone of Sangiovese, is trying to set itself apart from the crowd, but generally does not equal either Brunellos or Chianti Classicos in quality.

Tuscany is also the place that started the *vini da tavola* movement, and has consistently provided the most fertile hotbed for experimentation, discovery, and the free borrowing of ideas and techniques from winemakers around the world. The wines that have resulted are known as Super Tuscans, some of which rely in whole or in part on Cabernet Sauvignon, and others on Sangiovese. The most famous of these—Tignanello, Sassicaia, Sammarco and Solaia, among others—are now considered in a class with the top crus of Burgundy, Bordeaux and California.

Piedmont

With its own dialect, unique winemaking philosophy, and vintages that bear little correlation to the rest of Italy, Piedmont, in Northwestern Italy, is a world removed both culturally and enologically from the rest of Italy. Its best wines include Barolo and Barbaresco. Barolo, sometimes called the king of Piedmont reds, is made from 100 percent Nebbiolo; a wine of immense size and dimension, it demands cellaring, perhaps even more than the great wines of Bordeaux and Burgundy. Barbaresco is almost as long-lived and can be every bit as grand as Barolo, but is more supple and elegant, making it ready to drink a bit sooner.

Other good red wine choices include Nebbiolo d'Alba, which is fruitier and less forbidding than Barolo or Barbaresco and can offer exceptional value; Spanna, from the north of Piedmont, which can rival Gattinara from the same area at half the cost; and Barbera and Dolcetto, intended for early consumption and delicious in their youth.

Among whites, the Cortese—responsible for Gavi, Gavi di Gavi, and Cortese di Gavi—may be Italy's finest native white grape. Another fine Piedmont white is made from the Muscat-like Arneis grape. And Chardonnay is making an inevitable appearance here.

Other Wine Regions

While most of Italy's great wines still come from the familiar regions of Piedmont and Tuscany, wines from other areas are emerging on world markets. Here are some of the most promising:

Trentino-Alto Adige: This north-central region, spilling out of the Alps south of Austria, is internationally known for its Pinot Grigio and Chardonnay, and also produces the German varietals Gewürztraminer, Riesling and Sylvaner. The Merlot and Cabernet Sauvignon are also capable of world-class quality.

Friuli: The Collio region of Friuli has long produced subtly distinctive reds from Cabernet Franc and Merlot, with Cabernet Sauvignon sometimes added to the latter. Among whites, Pinot Grigio has always been taken quite seriously here, and is made in a dry, zesty style; Sauvignon Blanc and Tocai Friulano can also show power and intensity.

Veneto: Corvina is the predominant red grape in this region; its ultimate expression is Amarone, a monumental wine which requires drying the grapes on open racks to concentrate the flavors. Corvina is typically blended with other local grapes to produce Valpolicella and Bardolino, generally light wines which have the potential for far more intensity than is common. The same is true of the white Soave, made mostly from the Garganega and Trebbiano grapes.

Abruzzo: This promising region has been plagued by overproduction, but done well, Montepulciano d'Abruzzo (Montepulciano is the grape) can be similar to a Chianti.

Apulia: The signature red of this area in Italy's boot heel is Salice Salentino, a rich, often rustic red that can have real character. A lighter version called Rosso del Salento is also making a name for itself.

Sardinia: This island produces a refreshing white from the obscure Vermentino grape which is occasionally exported.

Portugal

Portugal's reputation as a great wine-producing country is based on its production of Port, a sweet wine fortified with brandy. In recent years, however, the quality and value offered by Portugal's dry, unfortified wines has become more appreciated.

Port

Although many imitations are produced around the world, true Port comes only from a designated part of the Douro region of Portugal, east of the city of Oporto. More than 80 different grape varieties are permitted to be used in Port, and several different types are often found jumbled together in the same vineyard. Among the chief black-skinned varieties are Tinta Barroca, Tinta Cão, Touriga Nacional, and Tinta Roriz (Spain's Tempranillo). A smaller amount of white Port is also made.

Vineyards of Quinta do Noval in Portugal.

There are three main styles of Port. Ruby Port is a young, bright red wine offering fresh fruit flavors; tawny Port, which may be aged for decades, features nutty, caramel-like flavors of great length and depth. These two types are called wood Ports because they are aged in wood barrels before bottling and thus are ready to drink when sold, requiring no further aging in the consumer's cellar. Both types are usually blends of different vintages.

The most revered Port is vintage Port. It is made only in the best years, when the grapes achieve a special ripeness and intensity. Most of its aging takes place in the bottle, often over a period of decades, in the cellars of collectors of this exquisite wine.

Dry Portuguese Wine

Portugal's best known dry wine is Vinho Verde, which literally means "green wine." Vinho Verde can in fact be red or white, as the "greenness" refers to the youth of the wine rather than its color. White Vinho Verde, made primarily from the Loureiro grape and less often the Alvarinho, is a fine apéritif wine. The red is often rough around the edges, and is seldom exported.

Portugal's best known dry wine region is the Dão. Two-thirds of Dão is red, and tends to age well; those marked Garrafeira (reserve) have been aged for a long time in wood and in bottle before being sold. The Douro valley in northern Portugal, the home of Port, is another source of some of Portugal's best red table wines, which are made from the same grapes as Port. Douro whites are generally less successful.

In recent years, other regions of Portugal have increased in prominence. The Barraida district, located between the Douro and the Dão, makes fairly highly extracted, Rhône-like reds principally from the indigenous Baga, but some experiments with Cabernet Sauvignon and Merlot have been impressive. Cabernet Sauvignon is also being planted alongside traditional varieties in the Sebutal district, until now best known for sweet, Muscat-based wine. Lastly there is the vast Alentejo region in Southern Portugal, known mostly for its light rosés and, more recently, potent, wood-aged reds.

Spain

Spain's top wines continue to be made with native grape varieties in traditional styles, but alongside these there is emerging a new breed of modern wines which are helping Spanish wine producers compete more successfully in the world arena.

Spain's wine laws are similar to those of the Italian system. Regulations governing the growing and making of wine apply to the various *Denominación de Origen (DO)* regions; an additional level (DOCA) with tighter restrictions was added in 1991, with Rioja the first region to qualify.

Table Wines

The most successful table wines in every price category are red, primarily those made from the Tempranillo grape, which dominates the regions of Rioja, Ribera del Duero, Navarra and Toro. Cabernet Sauvignon has begun to make an appearance, often blended with Tempranillo, while obscure local grape varieties contribute to the distinctive character of wines from Penedès, Priorato and Somontano.

Most wineries offer reds in four quality levels, which correspond to the amount of aging (in wooden barrels or in bottle) the wines receive before release. In order of increasing age (and price), they are:

Sin Crianza: Released in the year after harvest, these are light and rarely leave Spain.

The vineyards of Abadía Retuerta in Spain's Ribera del Duero region grow international varieties in addition to the traditional Tempranillo.

Crianza and Reserva: Both of these spend at least one year aging in oak barrels. They generally offer the best values and freshest fruit flavors.

Gran Reserva: Must spend at least two years in oak barrels, and are commonly released only five to seven years after harvest. Those who appreciate traditional wood-dominated, autumnal flavors and aroma find the best of these profoundly delicious.

These days white wines from Rioja and Rueda, made from the native Viura grape, frequently offer fresh citrus flavors in a modern style; many white Rioja reservas, on the other hand, are powerful examples of a traditional oak-aged style. Other good Spanish whites come from the Rias Baixas in Galicia, just north of Portugal, where the principal grape is the Albariño.

Cava and Sherry

Penedès is the most important source of *cava*, Spain's immensely popular sparkling wine. Indigenous grape varieties such as the Macabeo, Parellada and Xarello make up the bulk of *cava* blends, which can be fresh and fruity—and are generally much more affordable than Champagne.

Sherry is the fortified wine produced in and around the town of Jerez in southwestern Spain. It is made from white grapes, principally the Palomino; the wide range of color and body types—from *manzanillo* and

fino (at the lightest end) through *amontillado* to
oloroso—derives from an elaborate long-term aging
and blending process known as the *solera* system.
Note that all Sherry is dry in its natural state; unlike
Port, where sweetness is retained by adding brandy
to stop fermentation before it's complete, sweet
cream Sherries are made by blending in separate
sweet wine at the end of the process.

U.S.A.
California's Grape Varieties

California produces almost 90 percent of the wine
made in the U.S.A. Its greatest success has been in
the cultivation of classic European varietal grapes,
such as Cabernet Sauvignon, Chardonnay, Pinot Noir,
Merlot and Sauvignon Blanc. Along with France and
Italy, California is now regarded as one of the truly
great wine-producing regions of the world.

California wines are marketed primarily as varietals—wines made entirely or mostly from the single
grape variety (Chardonnay, for example) named on
the front label. (This differs from the classic
European approach, which is based primarily on geo-
graphic locations and/or appellations such as
Bordeaux or the Rhône.) The implications of this system are enormous. Instead of being limited to a few
grape types allowed under an appellation law,
California's winemakers have the flexibility to experiment when choosing what wines to make and how
to make them.

On the other hand, since California regulations do
require that at least 75 percent of a wine bearing a
varietal name be made from that varietal, winemakers
who wish to make complex blends (with no single
type contributing 75 percent) are left with the problem of what to call their fine wines. "Table wine" is
one legal option, but this risks confusion with inexpensive jug wines. Many wineries use proprietary
(trademarked) names; others use the word "Meritage"
for Bordeaux-style blends of specific grapes.

Among white wines, Chardonnay—the state's
most widely planted grape—and Sauvignon Blanc
are the major varietals. While many California

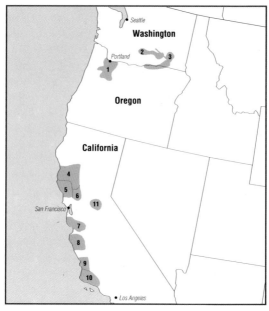

1. Willamette Valley
2. Yakima Valley
3. Columbia Valley
4. Mendocino & Lake Counties
5. Sonoma
6. Napa
7. Santa Cruz Mountains
8. Monterey County
9. San Luis Obispo
10. Santa Barbara County
11. Sierra Foothills

Chardonnays can be quite ordinary, the better ones are undoubtedly among the world's best. California Sauvignon Blanc is an often underappreciated and usually bargain-priced white. When blended with Sémillon it yields a rich style close to that of a white Bordeaux.

Cabernet Sauvignon is generally regarded as the king of California red wine. While some of the best California Cabernets are still made from 100 percent Cabernet Sauvignon, the trend in recent years has been to add Merlot and other varietals. Merlot, once thought of as a blending grape, has emerged as a hot new variety on its own; it's been called the "kinder, gentler" alternative to Cabernet Sauvignon. Another red, Pinot Noir, has had a checkered history in California, with many early examples lacking the expected elegance. But now it seems to have found a home in the state's cooler regions.

Zinfandel is the most widely planted red grape in California. It lends itself to an enormous range of styles, ranging from a rosé style called "white" Zinfandel at one extreme, to inky black late-harvest Zinfandels at the other. True red Zinfandel is usually a zesty, spicy wine. Other important varieties include some that originated in France's Rhône Valley, such as the reds Syrah and Mourvèdre and the white Viognier. A number of California winemakers, collectively called the "Rhône Rangers," are producing interesting wines from these grapes.

California's Wine Regions

Napa Valley is undoubtedly the best-known wine region of California. With more than 35,000 acres of vine planted today, Napa is able to produce a vast array of fine wines, and is particularly renowned for its Cabernets and Chardonnays. A number of sub-regions of Napa have developed individual winemaking identities, and several have been granted appellation status. These include Oakville, Rutherford, the Stags Leap District, Howell Mountain, Mount Veeder, and Spring Mountain.

Sonoma County is even more geographically diverse than the Napa Valley, and supports many grape varieties and wine styles. The historic heart of Sonoma County is the Sonoma Valley, where many of its oldest wineries are located. Sub-regions within Sonoma County include Alexander Valley, Dry Creek Valley, and Russian River Valley. Carneros, which straddles the southern ends of both Napa and Sonoma Counties, has developed a reputation for Burgundy-style wines made from Pinot Noir and from Chardonnay.

Other important regions in California are:

Lake County and **Mendocino County**, which lie just north of Napa and Sonoma. Sauvignon Blanc and Zinfandel thrive in the warmer inland areas, while Chardonnay, Pinot Noir and Riesling are grown close to the coast

The Santa Cruz Mountains, full of tiny, highly variable microclimates that produce a rich variety of distinctive wines.

Monterey County. Chardonnay is the standout varietal in the small appellations here: Carmel Valley, Arroyo Seco, and Chalone.

San Luis Obispo. The Paso Robles appellation, in the northern part of this county, is gaining a reputation for red varietals, especially Syrah, Zinfandel and Cabernet. In the south, Edna Valley specializes in Chardonnay, and Arroyo Grande in Chardonnay and Pinot Noir.

Santa Barbara County, including the Santa Maria Valley appellation in the north and the Santa Ynez Valley in the south; Chardonnay and Pinot Noir blends are also a specialty here.

The Sierra Foothills, especially Amador County, famous for its Zinfandels.

Other U.S. States

Three-quarters of Oregon's total wine production comes from the Willamette Valley, which stretches south from Portland in the northwestern part of the state. Oregon has shown a particular affinity for the Pinot Noir grape, and the leading examples are competitive with the best of Burgundy and California. Riesling and Pinot Gris are also successfully cultivated here.

Most Washington State wineries are located in the arid Columbia River Valley (which includes the smaller Yakima Valley and Walla Walla districts), east of the towering Cascade Mountains; the climate and viticultural conditions are very different from neighbor-to-the-south Oregon. Cabernet Sauvignon and especially Merlot do very well; whites include Sémillon, Sauvignon Blanc, Chardonnay and Riesling.

New York produces a great deal of wine, but the total includes a significant amount of wine made from native American grapes (such as the Concord and Catawba) and various hybrids, rather than the traditional European varietals. Fine-wine varietals which do thrive here include Merlot and Chardonnay (particularly on the North Fork of Long Island), and Riesling (in nearly all of the state's viticultural areas). Virginia, Texas and Idaho also produce notable amounts of quality wine.

Matching Wine with Food

The first thing to remember about matching food and wine is to forget the rules. Forget about shoulds and shouldn'ts. Forget about complicated systems for selecting the right wine to enhance the food on the table. This is not rocket science. It's common sense. Follow your instincts. The best advice is: Eat what you like and drink what you like. You'll find combinations that work, and they will suggest general rules that will increase your chances of creating other magical matches. And one day, when everything comes together—the food, the wine, the company—to create a whole that far surpasses any single element, you'll be glad you took the time and the effort to get the details right.

First of all, choose a wine that you want to drink by itself. Despite all the hoopla about matching wine and food, you will probably drink most of the wine without the benefit of food—either before the food is served or after you've finished your meal. Therefore, you will not go too far wrong if you make sure the food is good and the wine is, too. Even if the match is not perfect, you will still enjoy what you're drinking.

Some of today's food-and-wine pontificators suggest that mediocre wines can be improved by serving them with the right food. The flaw in that reasoning, however, is the scenario described above. If the match does not quite work as well as you hope, you're stuck with a mediocre wine. So don't try to get too fancy. First pick a good wine.

David Prince

The old rule about white wine with fish and red wine with meat made perfect sense in the days when white wines were light and fruity and red wines were tannic and weighty. But today, when most California Chardonnays are heavier and fuller-bodied than most California Pinot Noirs and even some Cabernets, color coding does not always work.

Red wines as a category are distinct from whites in two main ways: tannins—many red wines have them, few white wines do—and flavors. White and red wines share many common flavors; both can be spicy, buttery, leathery, earthy or floral. But the apple, pear and citrus flavors in many white wines seldom show up in reds, and the currant, cherry and stone fruit flavors of red grapes usually do not appear in whites.

In the wine-and-food matching game, these flavor differences come under the heading of subtleties. You can make better wine choices by focusing on a wine's size and weight. Like human beings, wines come in all dimensions. To match them with food, it's useful to know where they fit in a spectrum, with the lightest wines at one end and fuller-bodied wines toward the other end.

A Spectrum of Wines

To help put the world of wines into perspective, we offer the following lists, which arrange many of the most commonly encountered wines into a hierarchy based on size, from lightest to weightiest. If you balance the wine with the food by choosing one that will seem about the same weight as the food, you raise the odds dramatically that the match will succeed.

It's perfectly true that some Champagnes are more delicate than some Rieslings and some Sauvignon Blancs are bigger than some Chardonnays, but we're trying to paint with broad strokes here. When you're searching for a light wine to go with dinner, pick one from the top end of the list. When you want a bigger wine, look toward the end.

Bil Milne

*Selected dry and off-dry white wines,
lightest to weightiest:*

- Soave, Orvieto, Pinot Grigio
- Off-dry Riesling
- Dry Riesling
- Muscadet
- Champagne and other dry sparkling wines
- Chenin Blanc
- French Chablis and other unoaked Chardonnays
- Sauvignon Blanc
- White Bordeaux
- White Burgundy
- Pinot Gris (Alsace, Tokay)
- Gewürztraminer
- Barrel-fermented or barrel-aged Chardonnay
  (United States, Australia)

Selected red wines, lightest to weightiest:

- Valpolicella
- Beaujolais
- Dolcetto
- Rioja
- California Pinot Noir
- Burgundy
- Barbera
- Chianti Classico
- Barbaresco
- Barolo
- Bordeaux
- Merlot (United States)
- Zinfandel
- Cabernet Sauvignon (United States, Australia)
- Rhône, Syrah, Shiraz

More common sense: Hearty food needs a hearty wine, because it will make a lighter wine taste insipid. With lighter food, you have more leeway. Lighter wines will balance nicely, of course, but heartier wines will still show you all they have. Purists may complain that full-bodied wines "overwhelm" less hearty foods, but the truth is that anything but the blandest food still tastes fine after a sip of a heavyweight wine.

The moral of the story is not to let some arbitrary rules spoil your fun. If you like a wine, drink it with food you enjoy and you're bound to be satisfied.

Jon Wyand

Ordering Wine in Restaurants

Many people find ordering wine in a restaurant even more intimidating than buying in a retail shop. But it can also be a satisfying adventure leading to new discoveries.

At a fine restaurant, the sommelier (sew-mel-yay), or wine steward, can be your greatest ally. The more parameters you can provide, the easier it will be for the sommelier to match the wine to your tastes. You might ask your guests what type of wines they enjoy and then ask the sommelier for suggestions in that general category—say, a fruity Merlot, a powerful young Cabernet or a fully-mature Bordeaux.

James Baigrie

To subtly communicate your price range, point to two or three wines on the list and say, "I'm looking at these; what do you think about them, or do you have any other suggestions?"

The sommelier can also advise which wines complement specific dishes. The simplest approach is to describe which dishes your group intends to order and ask for a recommendation.

Caroline Kopp

If the restaurant has no sommelier, the waitstaff should be able to describe wines that pair well with your dish. When the staff isn't on the ball and the wine list is not inspiring, it may be time to order beer, spirits or iced tea.

Finding Great Wine Restaurants

You can find restaurants with exceptional wine lists—wherever you live or travel—in the dining section at winespectator.com.

The Serving Ceremony

The traditional serving ceremony is observed in many restaurants.

Presenting the Bottle

Before opening the bottle at your table, the sommelier or waiter will show you the bottle so you can verify that it is indeed the wine you ordered. Check the producer, vintage and type of wine.

Presenting the Cork

After opening a bottle, the sommelier will present you with the cork. Look at it for clues to the wine's storage and condition:

- The cork should be moist; this indicates that the wine has been stored properly.

- There shouldn't be any streaks of wine running the length of the cork; if there are, the wine may have overheated and expanded, breaking the cork's seal and allowing air into the bottle.

- The cork in a young wine should never be crumbly. This is not necessarily the case in a wine more than 25 years old.

Since it is possible to have a poor cork in a great wine, tasting the wine itself is the best way to judge its condition.

Tasting the Wine

The sommelier finally pours a small amount of wine into the host's glass. Examine the wine's condition.

- Glance quickly at the color. A pale orange color might indicate a problem in a young red, as would a dark amber color in a young white.

- Swirl and sniff the wine. The wine shouldn't smell musty, nor should it smell of vinegar.

- Taste the wine. Again, musty or vinegary flavors would be undesirable.

Returning a Bottle

Anything that puts you off about a wine—if it's corked or spoiled, or isn't as described—is reason to bring it to the attention of the sommelier. In a good restaurant, the sommelier will bring you a new bottle with no questions asked. If the sommelier tastes the wine and thinks it's fine, however, he or she could legitimately suggest you choose another wine.

Tipping

Many customers tip 20 percent on restaurant bills if the service is good or better. That should include moderately priced wines, but it's not necessary to include whopping wine bills in the calculation. If a sommelier has been particularly helpful, you could tip him or her directly—$10 or $20 for the high-priced bottle—then base the waiter's tip on the rest of the bill.

There are no accepted rules on the matter, though. Let your conscience—and the quality of the service—be your guide.

By the Glass

Restaurants increasingly offer more and better wines by the glass, providing low-risk options for experimenting with new wines. Look for tasting menus that pair a different glass of wine with each course.

James Baigrie

Restaurants known for their wines or those with high traffic will have no problem finishing a bottle the same night it is opened, when the wine is at its best, but it's safest to ask how long the bottle has been open. If it has been open too long and the fruit is faded, ask for a glass from a fresh bottle.

BYOB

Occasionally you may want to bring your own bottle, either because the restaurant has no liquor license or because you want to share a special wine. Establishments that do not serve wine often encourage diners to bring their own bottles so they don't lose business, and they won't charge a fee.

Among restaurants with wine licenses, some allow you to bring your own wine while others don't. Those that do allow it will most likely charge a corkage fee to cover the wine service and use of glasses. The fee generally ranges from $5 to $25 per bottle, and may be higher for oversized bottles.

Call ahead to ask about the restaurant's policy. In addition, check whether the wine you want to bring is on the restaurant's list; if it is, your bottle will not be welcome.

Acetic acid: All wines contain acetic acid, or vinegar, but usually the amount is quite small and not perceptible to smell or taste. Once the level reaches 0.07 percent or above in table wines, a sweet-sour vinegary smell and taste becomes evident, and at over 0.1 percent, it can become the dominant flavor and is considered a major flaw.

Acid: A compound present in all grapes. Acid preserves wine, imparts crisp, sharp flavors and helps prolong its aftertaste. There are four major kinds of acids—tartaric, malic, lactic and citric—found in wine.

Aeration: The process of letting a wine "breathe" in the open air, or swirling wine in a glass. It's debatable whether aerating bottled wines (mostly reds) improves their quality. Aeration can soften young, tannic wines; it can also fatigue older ones.

Alcohol: Ethyl alcohol, a chemical compound formed by the action of natural or added yeast on the sugar content of grapes during fermentation.

American oak: Increasingly popular as an alternative to French oak for making barrels in which to age wine. Often marked by strong vanilla notes, it is used primarily for aging Cabernet, Merlot and Zinfandel, for which it is the preferred oak. It's less desirable, although used occasionally, for Chardonnay or Pinot Noir. See also French oak.

Appellation: Defines the area where a wine's grapes were grown, such as Bordeaux, Gevrey-Chambertin, Alexander Valley or Russian River Valley. Regulations vary widely from country to country. In order to use an appellation on a California wine label, for example, 85 percent of the grapes used to make the wine must be grown in the specified district.

Appellation d'Origine Contrôlée AOC: The French system of appellations, begun in the 1930s and considered the wine world's prototype. To carry an appellation in this system, a wine must follow rules describing the area the grapes are grown in, the varieties used, the ripeness, the alcoholic strength, the vineyard yields and the methods used in growing the grapes and making the wine.

Balthazar: An oversized bottle which holds the equivalent of 12 to 16 standard bottles.

Barrel fermented: Denotes wine—usually white—that has been fermented in small casks (usually 55-gallon oak barrels) instead of larger tanks. Barrel fermentation increases body and adds complexity, texture and flavor to certain wine types.

Bin Number: See cask number.

Blanc de blancs: "White of whites," meaning a (sparkling) white wine made entirely of white grapes, such as Champagne made of Chardonnay.

Blanc de Noirs: "White of blacks," white (sparkling) wine made of red or black grapes. e.g. Champagne that is made from Pinot Noir or Pinot Meunier. The juice is squeezed from the grapes and fermented without skin contact. The wines can have a pale pink hue.

***Botrytis cinerea*:** A beneficial mold or fungus that attacks grapes under certain climatic conditions and causes them to shrivel, deeply concentrating the flavors, sugar and acid; called the "noble rot." Some of the most famous examples come from Sauternes (Château d'Yquem), Hungary (Tokay) and Germany.

Bottle Sickness: A temporary condition characterized by muted or disjointed fruit flavors. It often occurs immediately after bottling or when wines (usually fragile wines) are shaken in travel. Also called bottle shock. A few days of rest is the cure.

Bottled by: Means the wine could have been purchased ready-made and simply bottled by the brand owner, or made under contract by another winery.

Brut: A general term used to designate a relatively dry-finished Champagne or sparkling wine, often the driest wine made by the producer.

Cask Number: A meaningless term, sometimes used for special wines, as in Stag's Leap Wine Cellars Cask 23, but often applied to ordinary wines.

Chaptalization: The addition of sugar to juice before and/or during fermentation, used to boost sugar levels in underripe grapes and alcohol levels in the subsequent wines. Common in northern European countries, where the cold climates may keep grapes from ripening, but forbidden in southern Europe (including southern France and all of Italy) and California.

Charmat: Mass production method for sparkling wine. Indicates the wines are fermented in large stainless steel tanks and later drawn off into the bottle under pressure. Also known as the "bulk process." See also *méthode champenoise*.

Cold Stabilization: A clarification technique in which a wine's temperature is lowered to 32° F, causing the tartrates and other insoluble solids to precipitate.

Crush: Harvest season, when the grapes are picked and crushed.

Cuvée: A blend or special lot of wine.

Decanting: A process for separating the sediment from a wine before drinking. Accomplished by slowly and carefully pouring the wine from its bottle into another container.

Demi-sec: In the language of Champagne, a term relating to sweetness. It can be misleading; although demi-sec means half-dry, demi-sec sparkling wines are usually slightly sweet to medium sweet.

Early harvest: Denotes a wine made from early-harvested grapes, usually lower than average in alcoholic content or sweetness.

Enology: The science and study of winemaking. Also spelled oenology.

Estate-bottled: A term once used by producers for those wines made from vineyards that they owned and that were contiguous to the winery "estate." In the U.S. today it indicates the winery either owns the vineyard or has a long-term lease to purchase its grapes, and the winery and vineyard must be located in the same appellation.

Extra-dry: A common Champagne term not to be taken literally. Most Champagnes so labeled are sweet.

Fermentation: The process by which yeast converts sugar into alcohol and carbon dioxide, turning grape juice into wine.

Filtering: The process of removing particles from wine after fermentation. Most wines unless otherwise labeled are filtered for both clarity and stability.

Fortified: Denotes a wine whose alcohol content has been increased by the addition of brandy or neutral spirits.

French oak: The traditional wood for wine barrels, which supplies vanilla, cedar and sometimes butterscotch flavors. Used for red and white wines.

Grown, produced and bottled by: Means the winery handled each aspect of wine producing.

Half-bottle: Holds 375 milliliters or 3/8 liter.

Imperial: An oversized bottle holding 6 liters (the equivalent of eight standard bottles) of Bordeaux or other red wine.

Jeroboam: An extra-large bottle; the specific size varies according to what it contains. A Jeroboam of Champagne or other sparkling wine holds 3 liters, the equivalent of four bottles; one of Bordeaux or other red wine holds 4.5 liters (six bottles). (The 3-liter red-wine bottle is called a double magnum.)

Late harvest: On labels, indicates that a wine was made from grapes picked later than normal and at a higher sugar (Brix) level than normal. Usually associated with botrytized and dessert-style wines.

Lees: Sediment remaining in a barrel or tank during and after fermentation. Often used as in *sur lie* aging, which indicates a wine is aged "on the lees." Usually applies to whites. See also *sur lie*.

Maceration: The steeping of the grape skins and solids in the wine during fermentation. The alcohol acts as a solvent to extract color, tannin and aroma from the skins.

Made and bottled by: Indicates only that the winery crushed, fermented and bottled a minimum of 10 percent of the wine in the bottle. Very misleading.

Magnum: An oversized bottle that holds 1.5 liters.

Meritage: An invented term, used by California wineries, for Bordeaux-style red and white blended wines. Combines "merit" with "heritage." The term arose out of the need to name fine wines that didn't meet minimal labeling requirements for varietals (i.e., 75 percent of the named grape variety). For reds, the grapes allowed are Cabernet Sauvignon, Merlot, Cabernet Franc, Petite Verdot and Malbec; for whites, Sauvignon Blanc and Sémillon.

Méthode Champenoise: The labor-intensive and costly process whereby wine undergoes a secondary fermentation inside the bottle, creating bubbles. All Champagne and most other high-quality sparkling wine is made by this process. See also charmat.

Methuselah: An extra-large bottle holding 6 liters of Champagne; the equivalent of eight standard bottles.

Must: The unfermented juice of grapes extracted by crushing or pressing; grape juice in the cask or vat before it is converted into wine.

Nebuchadnezzar: A giant wine bottle holding 15 liters; the equivalent of 20 standard bottles.

Negociant (Negociant-eleveur): A French wine merchant who buys grapes and vinifies them, or buys wines and combines them, bottles the result under his own label, and ships them. Particularly found in Burgundy. Two well-known examples are Joseph Drouhin and Louis Jadot.

Noble rot: See Botrytis cinerea.

Nonvintage: Blended from more than one vintage, thus allowing the vintner to keep a house style from year to year. Common nonvintage wines include many Champagnes and sparkling wines, Sherry, and tawny and ruby Port.

Nouveau: A style of light, fruity, youthful red wine bottled and sold as soon as possible. Applies mostly to Beaujolais.

Phylloxera: Tiny aphids or root lice that attack grapevine roots. The disease was widespread in both Europe and California during the late 19th century, and returned to California in the 1980s.

Private Reserve: This description, along with Reserve, once stood for the best wines a winery produced, but in the absence of a legal definition many wineries use it or a spin-off (such as Proprietor's Reserve) for rather ordinary wines. Depending upon the producer, it may still signify excellent quality.

Produced and bottled by: Indicates that the winery crushed, fermented and bottled at least 75 percent of the wine in the bottle.

Rehoboam: Oversized Champagne bottle equivalent to 4.5 liters or six regular bottles.

Sur lie: Aging a wine "on the lees" is traditionally used in Chardonnay production.

Salmanazar: An oversized bottle holding 9 liters, the equivalent of 12 regular bottles.

Tannin: The mouth-puckering substance—found mostly in red wines—that is derived primarily from grape skins, seeds and stems, but also from oak barrels. Tannin acts as a natural preservative that helps wine age and develop.

Tartaric acid: The principal acid in wine.

Tartrates: Harmless crystals of potassium bitartrate that may form in wine casks or bottles (often on the cork) from the tartaric acid naturally present in wine.

Viniculture: The science or study of grape production for wine and the making of wine.

Vintage date: Indicates the year that a wine was made. In order to carry a vintage date in the United States, for instance, a wine must come from grapes that are at least 95 percent from the stated calendar year. See also nonvintage.

Vintner: Translates as wine merchant, but generally indicates a wine producer/or winery proprietor.

Vintner-grown: Means wine from a winery-owned vineyard situated outside the winery's delimited viticultural area.

Viticulture: The cultivation, science and study of grapes.

Yeast: Micro-organisms that produce the enzymes that convert sugar to alcohol. Necessary for the fermentation of grape juice into wine.

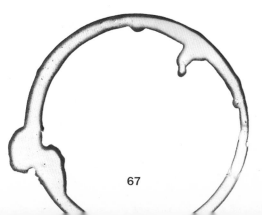

John Kuczala

Wine Spectator

2 0 0 5   V I N T A G E   C H A R T

(Updated January 2005)

Vintage charts are, by necessity, general in nature. Vintage ratings listed here are averages for region and year. For current vintages and exceptional older years, you will find our score and drinkability rating. A score range indicates that many wines of the vintage were not yet released at press time. "NYR" means not yet released.

100-Point Scale	
95–100	Classic
90–94	Outstanding
85–89	Very Good
80–84	Good
70–79	Average
60–69	Below Average
50–59	Poor

VINTAGE/SCORE/DRINKABILITY

ARGENTINA • Mendoza

2003	90-93	NYR
2002	93	Drink or hold
2001	87	Drink
2000	86	Drink
1999	90	Drink

CHILE • Red

2003	90-93	NYR
2002	88	Drink or hold
2001	92	Drink or hold
2000	87	Drink
1999	91	Drink or hold

FRANCE • Alsace

2002	90-94	Drink or hold
2001	93	Drink or hold
2000	93	Drink or hold
1999	87	Drink or hold
1998	90	Drink or hold

FRANCE • Bordeaux / Left Bank (Médoc, Pessac-Léognan)

2003	95-100	NYR
2002	88-91	NYR
2001	90	Hold
2000	99	Hold
1999	87	Drink or hold
1998	88	Drink or hold
1997	85	Drink
1996	91	Drink or hold
1995	96	Drink or hold

VINTAGE/SCORE/DRINKABILITY

FRANCE • Bordeaux / Right Bank (Pomerol, St.-Emilion)

2003	89-93	NYR
2002	86-89	NYR
2001	89	Drink or hold
2000	97	Hold
1999	85	Drink or hold
1998	95	Drink or hold
1997	86	Drink or hold
1996	87	Drink
1995	94	Drink or hold

FRANCE • Bordeaux / Older Reds

1994	85	Drink or hold
1990	97	Hold
1989	98	Hold
1988	93	Drink or hold
1986	94	Hold
1985	93	Drink or hold
1983	88	Drink
1982	96	Drink or hold

FRANCE • Burgundy / Red

2003	90-94	Drink or hold
2002	92-96	Drink or hold
2001	87	Drink or hold
2000	83	Drink or hold
1999	90	Drink or hold
1998	89	Drink or hold
1996	95	Drink or hold
1995	88	Hold

VINTAGE/SCORE/DRINKABILITY

1993	91	Drink or hold
1990	98	Drink or hold

FRANCE • Burgundy / White

2003	85-89	Drink or hold
2002	95	Drink or hold
2001	89	Drink or hold
2000	90	Drink or hold
1999	88	Drink or hold
1998	88	Drink or hold
1996	95	Drink or hold
1995	93	Drink or hold
1992	89	Drink or hold
1990	92	Drink

FRANCE • Champagne

1998	85-89	Drink or hold
1997	85-89	Drink or hold
1996	95	Drink or hold
1995	94	Drink or hold
1990	97	Drink or hold
1989	90	Drink or hold
1988	95	Drink or hold
1985	96	Drink or hold

FRANCE • Loire

2003	87-91	Drink or hold
2002	93	Drink or hold
2001	88	Drink
2000	86	Drink

FRANCE • Rhône / Northern

2003	92-96	NYR
2002	80	Drink
2001	89	Drink or hold

 Wine Spectator

Take the Guesswork Out of Buying Wine

Each issue of *Wine Spectator* magazine points you to the top wines, the best values and the most exciting producers. Our popular Buying Guide features ratings and tasting notes for more than 500 new releases, in every price range.

To subscribe to *Wine Spectator*, visit us online at **www.winespectator.com** or call **800-752-7799**

Vintage	Score	Drinkability
2000	88	Drink or hold
1999	96	Drink or hold
1998	89	Drink or hold
1996	90	Drink
1995	91	Drink
1990	97	Drink or hold

FRANCE • Rhône / Southern

Vintage	Score	Drinkability
2003	90-95	NYR
2002	78	Drink
2001	92	Drink or hold
2000	94	Drink or hold
1999	89	Drink
1998	97	Drink or hold
1995	90	Drink or hold
1990	95	Drink or hold
1989	96	Drink or hold

FRANCE • Sauternes

Vintage	Score	Drinkability
2003	92-94	NYR
2002	88-92	NYR
2001	97	Hold
2000	87	Drink or hold
1999	90	Drink or hold
1997	92	Drink or hold
1990	97	Drink
1989	98	Drink or hold
1988	93	Hold

GERMANY • Riesling

Vintage	Score	Drinkability
2003	90-94	Drink or hold
2002	93	Drink or hold
2001	98	Drink or hold
2000	82	Drink or hold
1999	90	Drink or hold
1998	89	Drink or hold
1997	88	Drink or hold
1996	89	Drink or hold
1990	97	Drink or hold

ITALY • Piedmont

Vintage	Score	Drinkability
2002	68-72	NYR
2001	92-96	NYR
2000	100	Drink or hold
1999	92	Drink or hold
1998	93	Drink or hold
1997	99	Hold
1996	98	Drink or hold
1990	97	Drink
1989	97	Drink
1988	92	Drink
1985	94	Drink

ITALY • Tuscany / Bolgheri & Maremma

Vintage	Score	Drinkability
2003	84-88	NYR
2002	85-89	Drink or hold
2001	96	Hold
2000	89	Hold
1999	93	Drink or hold
1998	98	Drink or hold
1997	97	Drink or hold

ITALY • Tuscany / Brunello di Montalcino

Vintage	Score	Drinkability
2002	84-89	NYR
2001	88-92	NYR
2000	85-90	NYR
1999	97	Hold
1998	91	Drink or hold
1997	99	Drink or hold

ITALY • Tuscany / Chianti & Chianti Classico

Vintage	Score	Drinkability
2003	85-90	NYR
2002	79	Drink
2001	92	Drink or hold
2000	88	Drink
1999	94	Drink or hold
1998	89	Drink
1997	97	Drink or hold

PORTUGAL • Vintage Port

Vintage	Score	Drinkability
2000	97	Hold
1997	96	Hold
1995	92	Hold
1994	99	Hold
1992	94	Drink or hold
1991	93	Drink or hold
1985	93	Drink or hold
1983	92	Drink or hold
1980	90	Drink or hold
1977	97	Drink or hold
1970	95	Drink or hold
1966	93	Drink or hold
1963	98	Drink or hold

SOUTH AFRICA • Red

Vintage	Score	Drinkability
2003	92-95	NYR
2002	84	Drink
2001	91	Drink or hold
2000	90	Drink or hold

SPAIN • Priorat

Vintage	Score	Drinkability
2002	85-89	NYR
2001	94-98	NYR
2000	92	Drink or hold
1999	91	Drink or hold

SPAIN • Ribera del Duero

Vintage	Score	Drinkability
2002	78-82	NYR
2001	92-96	NYR
2000	89	Drink or hold
1996	92	Drink or hold

SPAIN • Rioja

Vintage	Score	Drinkability
2002	80-84	NYR
2001	93-97	NYR
2000	86	Drink or hold
1995	92	Drink or hold

UNITED STATES

CALIFORNIA • Cabernet / Napa

Vintage	Score	Drinkability
2002	91-93	NYR
2001	93	Drink or hold
2000	85	Drink
1999	97	Drink or hold
1998	84	Drink
1997	99	Drink or hold
1996	96	Drink
1995	97	Drink
1994	97	Drink
1993	88	Drink
1992	93	Drink
1991	91	Drink
1990	89	Drink
1987	95	Drink
1986	96	Drink
1985	97	Drink

CALIFORNIA • Chardonnay / Carneros

Vintage	Score	Drinkability
2002	95-97	Drink
2001	93	Drink
2000	96	Drink

CALIFORNIA • Chardonnay / Napa

Vintage	Score	Drinkability
2002	92-94	Drink
2001	87	Drink
2000	87	Drink

CALIFORNIA • Chardonnay / Santa Barbara

Vintage	Score	Drinkability
2002	85-87	Drink
2001	89	Drink
2000	86	Drink

CALIFORNIA • Chardonnay / Sonoma

Vintage	Score	Drinkability
2002	97-99	Drink
2001	94	Drink
2000	89	Drink

CALIFORNIA • Merlot / Napa

Vintage	Score	Drinkability
2002	87-89	Drink or hold
2001	87	Drink or hold
2000	83	Drink
1999	87	Drink or hold

CALIFORNIA • Pinot Noir / Santa Barbara

Vintage	Score	Drinkability
2002	90-92	Drink or hold
2001	88	Drink or hold
2000	83	Drink
1999	82	Drink

CALIFORNIA • Pinot Noir / Sonoma

Vintage	Score	Drinkability
2002	92-94	Drink or hold
2001	88	Drink or hold
2000	85	Drink
1999	89	Drink

CALIFORNIA • Syrah / Napa

Vintage	Score	Drinkability
2002	98	Hold
2001	97	Drink or hold
2000	93	Drink or hold
1999	93	Drink or hold

CALIFORNIA • Zinfandel / North Coast

Vintage	Score	Drinkability
2002	86	Drink or hold
2001	87	Drink or hold
2000	81	Drink
1999	86	Drink or hold

OREGON • Pinot Noir

Vintage	Score	Drinkability
2002	97	Drink or hold
2001	94	Drink or hold
2000	91	Drink or hold
1999	94	Drink
1998	92	Drink